BLAZERS

TOP 10
UNEXPLAINED

TOP 10

MYTHICAL CREATURES

by Lori Polydoros

Content Consultant:
Dr. Andrew Nichols, Director
American Institute of Parapsychology
Gainesville, Florida

Reading Consultant:
Barbara J. Fox
Reading Specialist
Professor Emeritus
North Carolina State University

CAPSTONE PRESS
a capstone imprint

Blazers is published by Capstone Press,
1710 Roe Crest Drive, North Mankato, Minnesota 56003.
www.capstonepub.com

Books published by Capstone Press are manufactured with paper
containing at least 10 percent post-consumer waste.

Library of Congress Cataloging-in-Publication Data
Polydoros, Lori, 1968–
    Top 10 mythical creatures / by Lori Polydoros.
       p. cm. — (Blazers. Top Ten Unexplained) (Blazers. Animal Weapons and Defenses)
    Summary: "Describes various mythical creatures in a top-ten format"—Provided by publisher.
    Includes bibliographical references and index.
    ISBN 978-1-4296-7640-3 (library binding)
    1. Animals, Mythical—Juvenile literature. 2. Monsters—Juvenile literature. 3. Animals—
Folklore. I. Title. II. Title: Top ten mythical creatures. III. Series.
GR820.P65 2012
398.24'54—dc23
                                                                      2011034688

Editorial Credits
Mandy Robbins, editor; Veronica Correia, designer; Eric Gohl, media researcher;
    Laura Manthe, production specialist

Photo Credits
Alamy/AF Archive, 27; Photos 12, 19, 23
Fotolia/Ancello, 9 (front)
Newscom/akg-images, 7, 13; Itar-Tass Photos. 21
Shutterstock/Catmando, 11; Galyna Andrushko, cover (background), 9
    (background); Gian Corrêa Saléro, 25; Linda Bucklin, 17; Patalakha Serg, 28–29;
    Ruslan Kudrin, cover (front), 5
Svetlana Zhurkin, 15

Printed in the United States of America in Stevens Point, Wisconsin.
102011   006404WZS12

TABLE OF CONTENTS

MYSTERIOUS

Long ago, people thought up mythical creatures to help explain the mysteries around them. Today these creatures are found in books, movies, and TV shows. Count down today's top 10 mythical creatures!

mythical—imaginary or not real

LEVIATHANS

According to **Jewish** myths, leviathans were sea monsters. They had fins, fangs, and scales. These monsters were the gatekeepers of the **underworld**.

Jewish—describing Judaism, a religion based on a belief in one god and the teachings of a holy book called the Torah

underworld—the mythical place under the earth where spirits of the dead were once believed to go

HYDRA

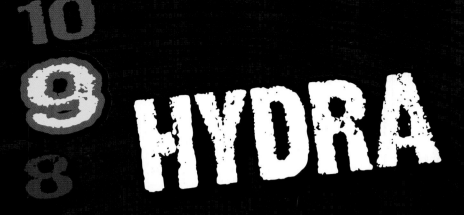

This water beast had many heads and poisonous breath. If the hydra lost a head in battle, two more would grow back. According to Greek myths, the hero Hercules eventually killed the hydra.

FACT The mythical hydra inspired the name for the freshwater creature called the hydra. This small animal has many limbs. If it loses a limb, another grows back.

PEGASUS

In Greek myths, this white, winged horse sent lightning and thunder to Mount Olympus. Today this flying horse lives on in many books and movies.

FACT In the popular Percy Jackson book series, the pegasus' name is Blackjack.

CENTAURS

According to Greek myths, a centaur was half-man and half-horse. Centaurs stood for the wild side of nature. Today they can be found in popular books and movies. Some examples are the Harry Potter and the Chronicles of Narnia series.

FACT

In one Greek myth, centaurs kidnapped a bride from her own wedding!

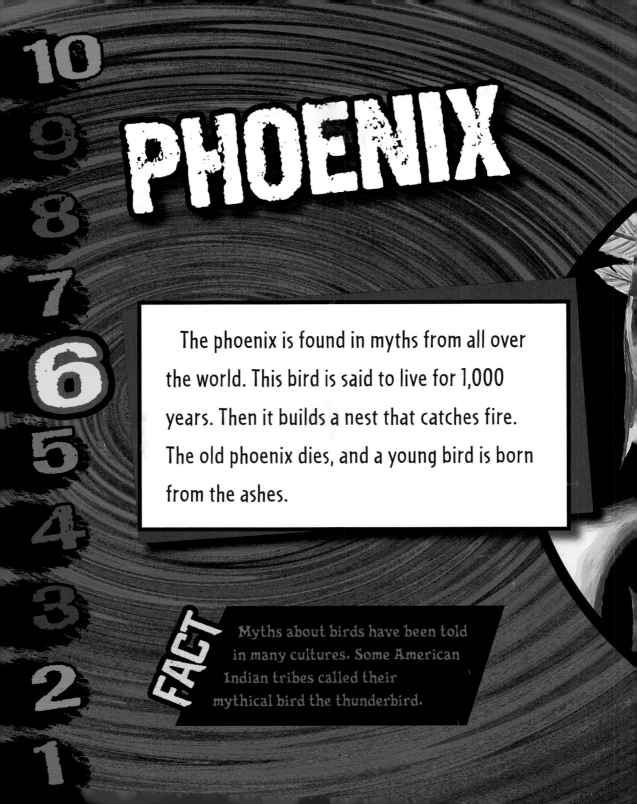

10
9
8
7
6
5
4
3
2
1

PHOENIX

The phoenix is found in myths from all over the world. This bird is said to live for 1,000 years. Then it builds a nest that catches fire. The old phoenix dies, and a young bird is born from the ashes.

FACT

Myths about birds have been told in many cultures. Some American Indian tribes called their mythical bird the thunderbird.

DRAGONS

Dragon tales have been told in many cultures. European dragons look like reptiles with wings. Chinese dragons look more like snakes. These fire-breathing beasts have battled brave warriors for hundreds of years.

FACT Stories about dragons may have started when people first found dinosaur bones.

ZOMBIES

For hundreds of years, **voodoo** followers have believed in zombies. According to voodoo teachings, priests cast spells on people. The people then appear to die and come back to life. These undead monsters are under the control of the priests.

voodoo–a religion that began in Africa and spread to Haiti and parts of North America

In movies, many zombies try to eat human brains!

19

10
9
8
7
6
5
4

2
1

WIZARDS

For many years, wizards were seen as old men who cast spells. Today wizards have been given a youthful twist. The Harry Potter books and the TV show *Wizards of Waverly Place* are about young wizards.

FACT According to legend, Merlin was a wise wizard who lived long ago. He helped King Arthur unite all of England in the 500s.

WEREWOLVES

Many stories tell of humans becoming werewolves from a bite or a **curse**. These people change into hairy beasts when the moon is full. Werewolves have super strength and speed. They also have an amazing sense of smell.

curse–an evil spell meant to harm someone

VAMPIRES

In the 1700s, people often died of mysterious illnesses. Europeans didn't understand how these illnesses were spread. They believed the dead were coming back to life as vampires to kill others.

FACT According to legend, driving a stake through a vampire's heart is one way to kill it.

10
9
8
7
6
5
4
3
2
1

Today vampires are popular characters in books, TV shows, and movies. The Twilight series pits vampires against werewolves.

FACT In 1897 Bram Stoker's novel *Dracula* made vampires popular.

ETERNAL LIFE

Today we know that mythical creatures aren't real. These creatures may never have existed, but they will live on in legends for years to come.

Glossary

curse (KURS)—an evil spell meant to harm someone

Jewish (JOO-ish)—describing Judaism, a religion based on a belief in one god and the teachings of a holy book called the Torah

legend (LEJ-uhnd)—a story handed down from earlier times; legends are often based on fact, but they are not entirely true

mythical (MITH-uh-kuhl)—imaginary or not real

series (SIHR-eez)—a number of works about the same subject

underworld (UHN-dur-wurld)—the mythical place under the earth where spirits of the dead were once believed to go

voodoo (VOO-doo)—a religion that came from East Africa with a mixture of Roman Catholic elements

Read More

Knudsen, Shannon. *Fantastical Creatures and Magical Beasts.* Fantasy Chronicles. Minneapolis: Lerner Publications, 2010.

Regan, Lisa, and Chris McNab. *Urban Myths and Legendary Creatures.* Monsters and Myths. New York : Gareth Stevens Pub., 2011.

Woog, Adam. *Zombies.* Monsters and Mythical Creatures. San Diego: ReferencePoint Press, 2011.

Internet Sites

FactHound offers a safe, fun way to find Internet sites related to this book. All of the sites on FactHound have been researched by our staff.

Here's all you do:

Visit *www.facthound.com*

Type in this code: 9781429676403

Super-cool stuff!

Check out projects, games and lots more at
www.capstonekids.com

Index